Thank you for picking up a copy of this book. I'm an independent author, and I wrote, designed, typeset, and published this book myself. It's a labor of love, and your support means a lot to me.

If you find this book thought-provoking or useful, here are the best ways to help me spread the word:

- Leave a review of the book on Amazon or Audible. Posting a review is quick and easy, and detailed reviews help new readers discover the book.
- Donate a copy to your local public library.
- Gift a copy to a friend or colleague who is starting something new, or in the midst of a significant change or transition.

I'd also love to hear from you if this book touches your life in some way. You can reach me via email at josh@howtofightahydra.com. Thanks for reading!

Josh

BOOKS BY

JOSH KAUFMAN

THE PERSONAL MBA

Master the Art of Business

personalmba.com

THE FIRST 20 HOURS

How to Learn Anything... Fast!

first20hours.com

HOW TO FIGHT A HYDRA

Face Your Fears, Pursue Your Ambitions, and Become the Hero You Are Destined to Be

howtofightahydra.com

HOW TO FIGHT A HYDRA

Face Your Fears, Pursue Your Ambitions, and Become the Hero You Are Destined to Be

JOSH KAUFMAN

Publisher's Cataloging-In-Publication Data
(Prepared by The Donohue Group, Inc.)

Names: Kaufman, Josh, author.

Title: How to fight a Hydra : face your fears, pursue your ambitions, and become the hero you are destined to be /Josh Kaufman.

Description: First edition. | Fort Collins, Colorado : Worldly Wisdom Ventures LLC, [2018] | Includes bibliographical references.

Identifiers: ISBN 9780979669507 (print) | ISBN 9780979669514 (ebook)

Subjects: LCSH: Conduct of life. | Uncertainty. | Ambition. | LCGFT: Allegories.

Classification: LCC BF637.S8 K38 2018 (print) | LCC BF637.S8 (ebook) | DDC 158.1--dc23

LCCN: 2018910349

This is a work of fiction. Any resemblance to actual events, locations, persons living or dead, or ravenous multiheaded serpentine monstrosities is coincidental.

First edition.
Typeset by the author on October 18, 2018.

FOR NATHAN

"The warrior and the artist live by the same code of necessity, which dictates that the battle must be fought anew every day."

STEVEN PRESSFIELD
author of *The War of Art*, veteran slayer of Hydras

CONTENTS

Author's Note 1

Translator's Preface 3

1 The Quest 5

2 The Journey 15

3 The Struggle 25

4 The Outcome 51

5 The Insight 61

6 The Decision 77

Afterword 89

Author's Commentary 91

Preparing for Your Adventure 101

Annotated Bibliography 105

Acknowledgments 112

Production Notes 114

About the Author 115

AUTHOR'S NOTE

Somewhere in the depths of your mind, a monster of a project is lurking.

It's big enough to scare you. Moving forward requires significant risk. Success is not guaranteed, and you're not confident you have what it takes to make it work.

How to Fight a Hydra is a story about summoning the courage to face the beast, fight the good fight, and persist long enough in your efforts to secure a lasting victory.

May it be a light in dark places when the future is uncertain or all seems lost.

Josh Kaufman
Fort Collins, Colorado, USA
September 2018

TRANSLATOR'S PREFACE

I discovered the following manuscript several years ago among the dusty shelves of a Bucharest antiquities dealer. The pages exhibited substantial water damage, and the scaled-hide casework and binding were in terrible shape, suggesting prolonged exposure to the elements.

Given the subject matter, we are fortunate the book exists at all, and that it has survived to the present day.

The original text is in Aromanian, a language similar to Romanian but with notable Greek influences. The author's name, age, gender, precise location, and date of writing is unknown, but the linguistic style and paper quality suggest a period between the late 11th to early 12th century CE.

I have updated the language and phrasing to make the text accessible to modern readers.

PART 1

THE QUEST

I have decided upon my purpose: I will slay a Hydra and claim its treasure, like the heroes of old.

Adventuring is dangerous, but if I continue my present course, I will go insane. I've had enough of sitting in a dusty room, hunched over a desk, my fingers cramped and stained with ink.

I'm not sure what calls to me about this particular ambition, but it is important to me. If I do not act, I consign myself to a life of regret.

For better or worse, I must do this.

Father and Mother think I am a fool.

"Our family is prosperous enough," they say. "Why go looking for trouble? Why chase fortune and renown? Why waste your training? Why gamble with your future? Why risk your life and well-being with no guarantee of success?"

My friends express similar concerns. "Be sensible. You are not Hercules. You are not a mighty warrior or a powerful sorcerer. This is a task for heroes, people of destiny. You're a scribe. What makes you think you can do this?"

When I told my master about my plans, he shook his head, then handed me another scroll to copy. "The legends have gone to your head. Do not desire what you cannot hope to accomplish."

I know why my loved ones do not support my choice: they are afraid. Afraid it will be a terrible decision. Afraid I will sacrifice much and gain nothing. Afraid I will come to harm, or die in the pursuit.

I cannot fault them. They do not know what will happen. Neither do I. That's the problem: so many uncertainties, so many anxieties, so many unknowns.

They are also afraid of what will happen if I succeed. What if I manage to kill a Hydra and become known throughout the land? What if I claim a vast treasure, surpassing their wealth and status? What if the experience changes me?

If I try, and they don't, what does that say about *them*?

I will persist. I have made up my mind, and I will follow through with my plans.

I accept the risks. What I am doing may not work. I might be wasting my time. I may end up worse off than I am now.

I cannot control the outcome of my quest. I can only control myself: how I prepare, how I manage my fears, and how I conduct myself in the battle to come.

What do I know about Hydras? Not as much as I'd like. I've never seen one with my own eyes.

Most of what I've heard comes from stories: from scrolls and books, tales told in taverns, and the songs of minstrels and bards.

In every case, the hero faces the beast with great courage and claims victory after a valiant and daring struggle.

I hope the stories are accurate.

According to the stories, what makes a Hydra fearsome is not its scaly hide, acrid stench, or row upon row of dagger-like teeth. It's the multitude of writhing, ravenous, serpentine heads.

Fighting a Hydra is not a battle with a single opponent: it's a battle with many opponents at the same time, all intent on introducing you to your doom.

When you cut off one of the Hydra's heads, legend says, it will grow two more unless you cauterize the wound with a torch. Hercules prevailed in this way, and I will follow his example.

What else can I discern about Hydras?

They must be rare. Otherwise, they would be seen hunting in the forests and rampaging through villages in search of food. They must make their homes in the deep, dark places of the world, beyond the borders known to ordinary folk.

My search must begin in the wilds, in caves and caverns. Where better for a monster to hide?

This is not appealing, but I must go to the Hydra: it will not come to me.

I have used the money I've earned in my apprenticeship to buy a simple but well-made sword and a whetstone. I have learned to make torches from lard and pine resin that will burn bright and long.

I will not trust my fate to unreliable tools.

I have also set myself to physical training. I must be strong enough to swing the sword with force, and quick enough to apply the torch while dodging the enemy's vicious strikes.

This training does not come naturally to me. The sword is heavy in my hand, and my footwork is too slow. I must work to improve.

I must also improve my strength and stamina. Endurance is necessary to win the battle. The fight will be exhausting, and I must be able to withstand fatigue and injury.

The ideal of fortitude extends to my mind and emotions as well.

I must learn patience, maintain my resolve, and develop the force of will required to see this job through to the end.

I am afraid.

That is not a reason to avoid the beast. Courage means being afraid and acting anyway.

I leave at dawn.

PART 2

THE JOURNEY

I have traveled into the wilds for the better part of a day now, searching for caverns in the foothills of the mountain forests.

I am alone, with only my horse for company. We pass beneath the canopy of evergreens in silence looking for openings in the rock.

I have my sword and a bundle of torches along with an old set of leather armor I've pieced together.

Beyond that, my saddlebags are light: a few days of rations, a waterskin, my traveling cloak, a bedroll, a waxed tarp, a coil of rope, a tinderbox, a few containers for lard and pine resin, a cook pot, my hunting bow, a quiver of arrows, and my field knife.

I also have my writing supplies and this book: a parting gift from my master. I'm writing this by the light of my campfire, a welcome rest after a long day in the saddle.

It would be nice to have more, but I'll manage.

A little before dawn, it began to rain.

I spent the entire day taking shelter under a pine tree, huddled next to my horse, shivering in the cold and damp.

It's too wet to start a fire, and the rations are gone.

I have been exploring the wilds for a week, and I have made no progress.

Every day is the same: I am forced to hunt and forage for food, which reduces the time I can spend searching for the Hydra.

I found a cave today, nestled in a small valley, its entrance concealed behind a thick hedge of brambles. It was shallow enough that light from the entrance reached the back wall, illuminating a hard floor and a scattering of moldering bones.

If this cave once held either a Hydra or a treasure, they're long gone.

Will I find what I seek? Am I doing the right thing? I can't be sure.

Should I keep going or turn back before it's too late?

What *is* this thing I'm doing, exactly? I'm no longer bound by the demands of daily life in town. I have no one to tell me what to do. There are no orders to follow, nor is there the promise of a reward for a job well done. It's difficult to tell if I'm even making progress.

I am wandering, but wandering with a purpose. I have an outcome in mind, but the future is impossible to know.

I suppose this is the essence of adventuring. You know what you want, but the only way you can get it is to abandon what you know, set off into the world, and trust in preparation, skill, and Fortune to see you through to a good end.

I have settled into a routine. In the morning, I eat, exercise, practice wielding my sword and torch, then pack up and search for a few hours.

After the day's travel, I forage, hunt, and collect pine resin and firewood. In the evening, I make dinner, render lard from the day's hunt, and make new torches.

The routine is comforting. I don't have to make new decisions about what to do each day. I've already decided, so I don't have to think: I can get straight to work.

At first, I found hunting and foraging discouraging. Once I understood that supporting my body is essential to victory, the chores no longer bothered me.

I've investigated a few more caverns, all of which contained nothing but rocks, mold, and a thick layer of bat droppings.

I've lost track of how long I've been traveling: it feels like an eternity. I've been able to find enough food and water to survive, but my spirits are getting lower by the day.

How long can I go on like this?

I have started talking to my horse. Iolaus doesn't have much to say, but he's an excellent listener.

My daily practice is working.

The sword no longer feels so heavy, and I'm becoming swifter and more surefooted.

I keep my blade sharp, and it no longer takes me so long to make torches in the evening.

A pack of wolves is following us from a distance. They prowl closer and closer as the sun sets, waiting for an opportunity to strike.

The only thing that keeps them at bay is a lit torch at dusk and my campfire at night. The howls keep me awake and shivering with terror in my bedroll.

Every time I'm tempted to complain about the difficulty and unfairness of life, I remind myself that I knew it was going to be hard before I left home, and that there is no victory without struggle.

I have to keep going and hope for the best.

The mountain wood is getting darker, shrouded in fog and overgrown trees. A thick carpet of green moss covers the ground, deadening the sound of our passage.

A ways back, the scent of death was overpowering, and it spooked Iolaus. I understand his anxiety: it is impossible to feel at ease in this godforsaken place.

It is difficult to see the path ahead, and there are thousands of places for danger to hide. We are alone and exposed, surrounded by the unknown.

At last: I have found it.

PART 3

THE STRUGGLE

The foul smell was my first clue to the Hydra's whereabouts. A gigantic predator must hunt large prey, whose remains would decay after the monster feasts. The putrid scent led to the mouth of a cave, a black chasm descending deep into the earth.

I spent hours standing at the entrance, listening. Eventually, I heard the unmistakable sound of something *enormous* moving in the darkness.

My search is over. Now the battle begins.

I have made my camp well away from the cave, in a sheltered niche next to the mountain. I don't think the Hydra roams far, but it seems prudent to maintain some distance.

As I stand outside the cave, I'm forced to admit: I *really* don't want to go in there.

I always have a reason to delay: I need to sharpen my sword. I need to make better torches. I didn't sleep well last night. I may be coming down with a sickness. It's too cold, too windy, too rainy.

All excuses designed to fool myself into avoiding the confrontation. Where is the courage I felt when I set out on this journey?

No more excuses. My fears are justified, but not useful: I will proceed, even though I still feel afraid.

This Hydra is not going to fight itself.

It took me three days to muster the courage to enter the cave.

I crept just inside the entrance, paused for a moment, then scrambled up the slope and sprinted back to my camp.

I must consider my first foray into the cave a success. I didn't fight, but I took a small step closer to the objective. That is progress, and I need every victory I can claim right now.

Today, I ventured a little further into the cave. From the light of my torch, I could see seven branching tunnels just beyond the mouth of the cave: one huge central opening and three narrow passages on each side.

There are stalactites and stalagmites everywhere, many damaged, with fragments littering the damp stone floor. Water drips from the ceiling. The air is cold and thick with humidity.

The cave is not pleasant. The stench is overwhelming, and I expect to be eaten at any moment.

I am drawing a map on a piece of paper torn from the back of my book so I can plan.

Last night, I woke in a panic: something huge moved in the darkness, beyond the light of my campfire.

Iolaus, still hitched to a tree, was agitated, pacing back and forth. I scrambled for my weapons and put my back to the mountain, my body alert and full of frantic energy.

Minutes passed. The only thing I could hear was Iolaus's anxious pacing, the crackling of my fire, the wind howling through the trees, and my heart pounding in my chest.

Eventually, Iolaus calmed and I put away my sword and torch. I tried to go back to sleep, but I couldn't.

I was still awake when dawn arrived.

After breakfast, I made my way to the cave. There were new scratches along the cave walls and damage to the stalagmites that wasn't there the day before.

The central tunnel was too large for stealth: I would be exposed and vulnerable. I decided to explore the rightmost passage first, careful to avoid making any sound. It was relatively narrow, but tall enough to stand in and about an arm-span wide.

The tunnel had many twists and turns, with several openings in the ceiling to larger chambers above, with water dripping down the mold-encrusted walls.

The passage made a sharp turn to the left. I peered around the corner and had to stifle a gasp.

There it was, a stone's throw away.

I crept closer to the monstrosity to get a better look. The Hydra had a mass of serpentine heads, which seemed to be asleep. Each head had a corresponding neck attached to the front of its reptilian torso, which was supported by four powerful legs. A thick, scaled tail extended back into the darkness.

I retreated to the mouth of the cave, then down the leftmost passage to view the beast from a different angle and get a better sense of its size.

The Hydra wasn't as gigantic as I imagined it would be. Darkness and fear had played tricks on my mind. In the torchlight, I could see that it was large and powerful, but not invincible.

The bones of large animals littered the ground, many of them fresh. I was fortunate: the Hydra was sleeping off its meal from the night before.

I inched my way along the wall, trying to get a glimpse of the back of the cave.

Would it be possible to claim the treasure while the Hydra sleeps and avoid a confrontation altogether?

The Hydra was blocking the depths beyond: I would have to climb over it to proceed. I was tempted to try, but thought better of it. The risks were significant, and the gain was too uncertain.

My mind full of thoughts of treasure, I stopped paying attention to my surroundings. My ankle turned on a stone, and I cried out in pain as I fell to the cave floor.

Six pairs of eyes snapped open, gleaming orange in the torchlight. Six serpentine heads rose to look in my direction.

The Hydra was upon me in an instant, jaws snapping, heads competing with each other for the kill.

I scrambled to my feet and sprinted back to the narrow passage, ignoring the pain from my ankle. Somehow, I made it to the opening without being swallowed.

The tunnel was large enough for only one of the Hydra's heads. They fought with each other for position until one managed to push its way inside. The Hydra's maw snapped and snarled, teeth glistening with saliva and acid. I backed away, raising my sword and torch, preparing for the worst.

As it lunged for me, I lashed out with my sword, which made a deep cut along its snout. Without hesitation, I thrust the torch toward the Hydra, a maneuver I had practiced hundreds of times. The fire didn't make contact, but the Hydra recoiled from the flames, and I fled down the tunnel.

I managed to escape the cave before the beast could catch me. Sometimes it is good to be small: you can move faster than the behemoth.

What have I learned from this encounter? I have faced the monster, and I have survived. I have struck my first blow. I know my enemy, and I know its weakness: it is afraid of fire. That is why it did not hunt me that night: my campfire kept me safe.

I will put a few extra logs on the fire tonight.

I have ventured into the cave once more, and I have learned another secret. Legends say that Hydras heal quickly. That's misleading.

It seems Hydras only regenerate when a head is cut off completely. The cut I made yesterday is still there and appears to be healing slowly.

That presents an opportunity. I will wage battle for a while, then withdraw to rest and recover. The following day, I'll be back to full strength, but the Hydra will be weaker than it was the day before.

I don't have to overpower it: I can outlast it.

I am still afraid, but less so than before. I have seen the enemy, I know the terrain, and I have a plan of action.

It is still a difficult task, but I can see the path to victory, and that gives me hope.

I have my hunting bow: perhaps I can shoot it through the heart?

I must try: any chance of a swift victory is worth testing.

No luck: my shot was accurate, but the arrow bounced off the Hydra's scaly torso, splintering on the cavern wall nearby.

It was a worthy experiment, but it cost me a valuable arrow, and the result is clear. I can't kill the beast from a distance.

Still, I am glad I tried: this information is valuable and could be learned no other way.

I must take the direct approach.

The Hydra's heads are always moving, always shifting, confusing and overwhelming. I can't hope to fight all of them at once. The only way to make progress is to isolate a single head long enough to make a successful attack.

I will use the environment to my advantage. I can lure one of the heads down a narrow side tunnel, then strike from a position of strength. It is my best chance.

Iolaus agrees that it is a very good plan.

Today's work was a resounding success.

I was able to surprise the Hydra, attract its attention from a distance, and lure it down a side tunnel. A single head pursued me, as before, and I was able to climb up into a vaulted chamber before it struck.

The head passed below me, exposed and vulnerable. I struck, slicing the neck clean through, and followed quickly with the torch to cauterize the stump. The Hydra's remaining heads roared in pain, and the beast retreated into the depths of the cave.

For the first time since I set out on this adventure, I feel like a proper hero.

Every once in a while, my fear recedes, and I have a glimpse of transcendence. The world fades, my mind is quiet, and all that exists is the task at hand.

I am feeling confident in my progress. A few more days of battle and it will be over.

The Hydra is learning. I tried the same approach I used yesterday, and it did not follow me.

I have found a few more hidden passages that I can use to isolate one of the Hydra's heads. They are my best chance. I must strike down one head at a time and keep going until the work is done.

It is clear the Hydra is tired, but it is also wary of my tricks and is getting more ferocious. It has not fed in many days.

I am also tired. I must take some time to rest, but not too long. Every day that I delay, the Hydra grows stronger.

A close call: I cut and cauterized another head, and the Hydra turned to flee. As I jumped down from my perch to watch it retreat, its tail whipped around, striking me in the torso.

The force of the impact threw me against the wall, and I bashed my head against the stone.

It's a good thing the Hydra was retreating: I was dazed and disoriented, too stunned to move. My body is bruised, and my head is still aching from the impact.

I must be more careful.

I have thought of another approach worth testing: if eating makes the Hydra sleep, perhaps I can give it something to feed upon, then strike as it slumbers.

I harvested a wild boar, then left the carcass at the mouth of the cave just before dark. With any luck, it will not be there in the morning.

It worked. Well-fed, the Hydra was sleeping soundly, and I took full advantage of the opportunity. Three heads down, three to go.

This method of fighting does not resemble the stories. When will I be skilled enough to face the monster like a champion, with no need for stealth or careful planning?

Disaster: after setting up another ambush, I did not apply the torch quickly enough, and the Hydra regrew two heads. Now I must sever four heads to complete the task, seven in total.

I must be patient with myself. I will make mistakes, and I can't predict the future or change what happened. The only thing I can do is learn by trial, and try to do better in the future.

I almost died today.

As I was making my way down a passage, the Hydra sprang from the shadows of a side chamber, catching me by surprise. Wicked teeth punctured my armor, and its mighty jaws closed around my torso.

I attacked the exposed neck by instinct and severed the head that held me. The torch followed, searing the stump and forcing the Hydra to retreat. I extracted myself from the Hydra's dead jaws and crawled out of the cave, barely conscious.

My wounds are severe, and the pain is unbearable.

My injuries are not healing, and the pain is getting worse. I can't fight in this condition. It is a struggle to hold this pen.

My wounds are inflamed and turning green with decay. My body is burning, covered in sweat and blood.

I need medicine and clean bandages. I do not have any in my saddlebags.

I must do *something*, or I will not survive the night.

I am using strips of my cloak to make bandages, boiling them in the cook pot, then packing them in my wounds. It's better than nothing: at least I can move a little, without prompting a fresh torrent of blood and decay.

There is also the dark green moss growing on the ground close to my camp. I am desperate: can I use it as a bandage?

Will it heal me or poison me? I can't be sure.

Unless I do something, I am dead. It is worth a try: if the moss harms me, I won't be any worse off than I am now.

Fortune smiles upon me: I'm still alive.

The moss is working. The fever has passed, my wounds are closing, and I am growing stronger every day.

I am well enough to hunt and forage. I must recover my health before facing the enemy once more.

I harvested a deer, and left it in front of the cave. Even though I'm improving, I do not want the Hydra to hunt me tonight.

Patience. I must keep my goal in mind, but act with prudence. Better to wait until the wounds heal over before I strike out again.

If I act before I'm ready, I risk permanent harm.

I have realized the error of my previous thoughts. The champions of antiquity were not stupid enough to face these monstrosities fully exposed, without advance planning or working to place themselves in an advantageous position.

As stories are told, feats of prowess are embellished, and the mundane reality of the struggle is left out to make the telling more exciting.

The heroes of legend did not slay the abomination in an hour, then return to their homes in time for dinner. It was just as difficult for them as it has been for me.

This truth is not obvious, but it is important, and it helps to know it.

Today I entered the cave for the first time in weeks. I have a new respect for my foe: it has harmed me, but I am still fighting. I will not stop until my task is done.

I have persisted with my strategy, and have managed to excise two more heads. Only one remains.

If all goes well today, I will accomplish my goal. May Fortune smile upon my efforts.

My sword bit deep, my torch burned hot, and my footing was solid and sure. The final head landed at my feet and the carcass fell to the earth, never to rise again.

The mighty Hydra, terror of the dark, has fallen to my persistent effort.

At long last, I am victorious.

PART 4

THE OUTCOME

After a brief rest, I made my way to the back of the cave.

Torchlight gleamed off a large pile of lustrous stones, hidden behind a boulder.

I approached. My breath caught in my throat.

It wasn't a horde of gemstones, as I first thought: just a small pile of worthless crystals.

I sank to my knees on the stone floor, tears wet upon my face.

I sat in the cave beside the corpse for a long time.

I had finally managed to slay a Hydra, but there was no treasure to claim. The hardship, the struggle, and the wounds had all been for nothing.

My parents and friends were right: I was a fool, pursuing foolish dreams. The legends were exaggerated, a collection of stories told to children to entertain them on rainy afternoons. Why did I assume the tales were true?

I stood and forced myself to start walking. It would be a long journey home, and breaking camp would provide a distraction from despair. If I kept myself moving, I could be half a day's ride closer to town by nightfall.

As I reached the mouth of the cave, I remembered a lesson: examine your environment and circumstances, and see if there's anything you can use to your benefit. What could I do? What could I try?

There was only one resource: a dead Hydra. What could I do with it?

I went back into the cavern and examined the carcass in more detail.

Seven serpentine heads, fearsome to behold. An enormous scaled hide, strong enough to turn away arrows. Row upon row of wicked teeth, sharp and long.

The Hydra wasn't *guarding* a treasure: it *was* the treasure.

I skinned the Hydra using my knife, taking care to avoid ripping the scaly hide. I coated three of the beast's heads with pine resin to preserve them, wrapped them in the skin, and strapped them to Iolaus's back with tough strands of the Hydra's sinew.

That done, I pried a long, serrated tooth from one of the other heads with the blade of my sword, and tested its sharpness and durability. The fang was capable of carving deep gouges in the stone floor without being damaged.

I removed each fang from the remaining skulls and placed them in my saddlebags.

The journey home will take time. I walk beside Iolaus, who sways under the weight of the Hydra's remains.

As we travel, I have continued my daily routine, with minor modifications.

Instead of making torches, I am working on a new set of Hydra-scale armor using my old pieces as a pattern. In the evenings, I use my knife to shape a Hydra's tooth, sharpening the edges and carving a handgrip in the base of the spike. It will make a fine dagger.

I have never done this work before. It's interesting, and I'm learning.

When I returned home, I was welcomed as a hero.

My parents were proud, my master was surprised, and my friends boasted of my accomplishments to anyone who would listen.

I enjoyed the attention and company for a while, but after a few weeks, it began to wear on me. I no longer needed validation or assurance: the struggle gave me everything I was looking to obtain.

My first adventure brought me a measure of wealth and renown. The Hydra's hide sold for a handsome price to the village armorer, and the sinew made for excellent bowstrings.

The Hydra's preserved heads have a place of honor on the wall of the village tavern, and minstrels sing songs of my exploits to eager crowds.

In the stories, I am fearless, confident, and self-assured. The battle is over in a day, and my success was foretold from the beginning.

A few weeks later, I saw the son of a wealthy merchant strutting around town in a brand-new set of Hydra-scale armor.

It looked silly on him.

One beautiful autumn morning, a few months after I came back to the village, I set off on a new quest. I was getting restless.

It was time to face the Hydra once more.

PART 5

THE INSIGHT

Since my first adventure, I have faced many more Hydras. This journal has accompanied me on each foray. It reminds me of how I started and how far I've come since the day I first set off into the wilds.

After each battle with the Hydra, I had hoped the next would be easier. It wasn't. This line of work is worthwhile, but it is never easy.

I will attempt to write down the lessons I have learned while adventuring so that I can avoid repeating unnecessary mistakes.

I am not sure if I will succeed: many important lessons are difficult to put into words, and the passage of time makes hard-earned wisdom easy to forget.

I've seen the lack of adventuring destroy more souls than a Hydra ever will.

For every adventurer who has been defeated by a Hydra in combat, thousands have been defeated by their own minds and refuse to face the Hydra at all.

The world is full of caverns. How can you know which ones hold treasure?

You can't know for sure, but there are clues.

The shallow caves you can see into from the outside don't contain anything worthwhile. They're too easy: anything they once held is long gone.

You're looking for a deep, dark, ominous cavern: something that scares you.

There's no sense in fighting with a dull, rusty sword.

Invest your gold in well-forged weapons. Keep your sword sharp, your torches ready, and your armor well-maintained.

Take care of your tools, learn how to use them, and they'll serve you well.

Hydras are revolting. They're ugly. They stink. They try to eat you. If you're looking for pleasant company, I can't think of a worse companion.

The Hydra's nature makes the prospect of adventuring even less attractive. Set aside the terror and the risk: almost anything else in the world is more enticing than facing the beast.

When you set out to face the Hydra, you will feel fear. No matter how many monstrosities you slay, you will experience anxiety, trepidation, and a sense of dread as you approach the cave.

Fear doesn't mean you're weak: it means you're *sane*.

Unpleasant emotions do not dictate your actions.

Many novices claim to be adventurers but never quite get around to standing toe-to-maw with the beast. Instead, they say to themselves, "I don't feel like it. Maybe tomorrow."

Always tomorrow. Always later. Always any time but *right now*.

You're facing a monster. Of course you "don't feel like it." Strap on your armor anyway.

Your mind can invent horrors beyond those that actually exist. Rumination is not your friend. Action allows you to see the situation for what it really is.

You're afraid that you're not good enough to handle what Fortune and happenstance have in store for you. You're afraid it's all going to go wrong and all of your efforts will be for naught.

You're afraid tomorrow will be the day you die.

The root of all fear is the unknown and unknowable future, which cannot be predicted or controlled.

Fear of the unknown will always be with you, no matter what you do. That's comforting in a way: if there's nothing you can do to change it, there's no reason to let it stop you.

Some attacks will hit. Others will miss. You can't predict which will be which in advance. You have to commit to every attack with the same intention: to strike the enemy.

That is the essence of battle. You cannot change it.

Setbacks, mistakes, and bad days are normal. There will be long periods where you don't know what to do or if you're doing the right thing.

That doesn't mean you're broken: it means you're human.

Adventuring requires trust in your own skills, judgment, and resilience. That's the primary benefit of experience. Every time your mind conjures doubts about your ability to handle chaos and strife, the memory of past experiences can provide an arsenal of counter-examples strong enough to overcome your fears.

Think back to all of the times you've struggled, adapted, and prevailed. You've done it before: you will do it again.

Risk is an unavoidable part of adventuring. A single mistake, made out of ignorance or carelessness, can kill you.

Only a fool relies solely on their resilience to mitigate damage. It's far better to learn to anticipate incoming strikes and not be there when they arrive.

The wise adventurer spends just as much time learning how to evade being hit as they invest in improving their skill with the sword and torch. Treasure isn't valuable if you're not around to enjoy it.

Wisdom consists of anticipating and preventing avoidable mistakes.

No matter how careful you are, you will make mistakes. After every engagement, there will be a hundred things that, looking back, you could've done better.

Since that's the case, the best approach is to make *valuable* mistakes: experiments that give you useful information and help you improve.

Over the course of your adventuring career, you'll earn more than a few battle scars. That's fine, as long as you expect it.

The novices who quit are the ones who think this profession is all glory and heroics. They're the ones who experience the dire consequences of foolish risks or give up the moment they take a scratch.

Knowing it's going to be difficult makes it easier to keep going.

A funny thing happens after you win your first victory: all of a sudden, you have something to lose.

The townsfolk have heard of your previous exploits. You have more treasure in your coffers. Everyone expects "great things" from you in the months and years to come. The next time you sally forth, all of these things will be in the back of your mind, along with a new fear:

What if I fail this time? What will people think of me if I fall or return with nothing?

It's best to put all thoughts of renown and reputation aside before you engage. The fight is difficult enough as it is.

The only thing worse than fighting a Hydra is fighting more than one Hydra at the same time.

The moment you prove you're capable of slaying a Hydra, everyone will have thoughts about who you are, what you're capable of, and how you should do your job. You'll hear an endless stream of commentary and advice from people who have never picked up a sword with intent.

Only take advice from people who have faced the beast.

Your confidence grows with every successful venture. Unless you're wary, it's easy to develop the mistaken impression that you cannot fail.

That's when you start to neglect all of the simple things that made you successful in the first place. You make beginner's mistakes, and those mistakes can be significant enough to end you.

Confidence is a potent ally, as long as it's tempered with wisdom and restraint. You're not invincible or infallible, so don't pretend to be. On the other hand, you're no longer a novice. You've earned the right to trust your own judgment and capabilities, even when others disagree.

There's a middle path between humility and hubris: work to find it.

A hero is born every time someone picks up a sword and torch, buckles on their armor, and decides to face their fears head-on, trusting in preparation and skill to see them through to victory.

Everyone wants a guaranteed reward before they put themselves at risk. The world does not work that way.

Not everyone succeeds. No matter how much you plan or prepare, a good portion of the outcome will remain in the hands of Fortune and happenstance. Generations have railed against this reality to no avail.

On the other hand, you can't succeed if you never try. Fortune tends to smile on those who *act*, even when the final outcome is not guaranteed. At some point, you must choose to move forward, do what you can, and hope for the best.

No one adventures forever.

There will come a day when you don your armor and unsheathe your sword for the last time. When that day comes, face it with courage and a clear mind.

Ending a chapter of your life on your own terms is a feat worthy of respect and admiration.

PART 6

THE DECISION

Early this morning, a group of eight travelers appeared at my door, the hoods of their cloaks pulled up to ward off the morning fog. I invited them in and put on a kettle for tea.

After exchanging pleasantries and introductions, they explained the purpose of their visit: they were a party of adventurers setting off to slay a dragon in a distant land, and I was invited to join them.

"We can use a hero of your caliber," they said. "It is rumored that the dragon sleeps on a mountain of gold and jewels. There will be more than enough treasure to make us all wealthy for a hundred lifetimes."

We talked for a long time, and I asked many questions.

They are well prepared, with beautiful horses, well-made armor, and excellent weaponry. They've acquired the necessary supplies and a map to guide them. Their leader seems trustworthy and competent, having led many similar excursions in her long adventuring career.

Everyone in the group is experienced and boasts of their previous exploits: staking vampires, hunting werewolves, banishing demons, and defending entire villages against hordes of the living dead. Each member of the party is confident that, together, they are more than a match for any dragon.

I thanked them for their invitation and told them I would consider their offer.

The leader of the party told me they can spare a day to await my decision, but cannot linger: the journey ahead is long and will continue in the morning, with or without my help.

What to do?

There is no doubt why they approached me: my reputation is well earned. I am experienced in this sort of work and have valuable skills to offer. The party is well organized and capable of the task. The rewards for success are considerable, beyond anything I've ever hoped to achieve.

Even so, this offer makes me hesitate.

I have made a life in this village. My home and family bring me great joy. If I join the party, I will be gone for months, possibly years. The risk is great: no matter how skilled or formidable you are, only a fool would choose to face a dragon on a whim.

I have until dawn to decide.

My adventures have resulted in material prosperity and the respect of the townsfolk. I have a family and many close friends. I live a comfortable life in a manner that suits me.

Now I am asked to give those up hard-earned treasures in exchange for a chance to become a legendary dragon-slayer: famous well beyond the borders of my small village and wealthy beyond measure. If the venture succeeds, generations will know my name and hear of my courageous deeds.

Is the opportunity worth the price?

I discussed the offer with my family.

"We don't need a mountain of gold and jewels," they said. "We'd rather you stay here and not take unnecessary risks."

Didn't my family, friends, and master tell me the same thing, just before I set out on the path that led to victory?

Do heroes decline when they are called to adventure?

I opened the lacquered wooden chest that contains my sword and armor and sat looking at them for a very long time.

Who am I? Who do I *want* to be?

It is midnight, and sleep is impossible.

I needed to persist in my first battle to prove to myself that I was capable. That is no longer in doubt. I have learned to choose my battles with care, and not hesitate to remove myself from situations where the circumstances are not to my advantage.

I did not choose this new adventure: it was offered to me. I never once considered hunting dragons until this morning. Dragons are crafty beasts, intelligent and wary. The thought of confronting one is not enticing.

Is this a once-in-a-lifetime opportunity, or an unnecessary distraction? Are the circumstances of this venture actually to my advantage?

If I accept this invitation, will I come to regret giving up everything I value to pursue someone else's dream?

If I decline and the party succeeds, will I regret my choice? How will I react if I learn that I was offered a chance at lasting glory but didn't have the nerve to take it?

Is my caution a sign of wisdom, or am I just scared?

Some Hydras exist only in the mind. I must claim victory over this one before first light.

The sky was crimson as I made my way to the inn an hour before sunrise.

I was dressed in my armor, my sword and dagger on my hip. Iolaus walked with an easy gait, his gray coat a dusty pink in the dim morning light. My saddlebags were full.

The adventurers were preparing to depart, loading their horses with supplies. As I approached, they turned to me, smiling.

I spoke, my voice clear and firm.

"Thank you, friends, for inviting me to join your venture. It is an unexpected honor."

I opened my saddlebags.

"I must decline your offer: my place is here, with my loved ones. I have brought each of you a gift. Consider it a token of thanks for your confidence and trust in me."

I handed every member of the party a dagger, carved by my own hand from a Hydra's tooth, encased in a leather sheath. The engravings on each bone-white hilt glowed in the light of dawn.

As I moved among them, I could see that several of the adventurers wore brand-new sets of Hydra-scale armor, and their bows were set with familiar bowstrings.

I smiled.

"I wish you every success. Farewell, and good luck."

The group was silent as I drew my sword, gave them a salute, then turned Iolaus toward home.

I arrived just as the sun crested the horizon, bathing the world in radiant light.

I brushed Iolaus, then left him to enjoy an extra helping of feed and an apple. My family was still asleep, the house quiet and peaceful.

I took off my armor and placed it carefully into the wooden chest. I set my sword on top of the breastplate, then closed the lid.

With a clear mind and a light spirit, I locked the chest. The sun was rising, and it was time to make breakfast.

AFTERWORD: A CALL TO ARMS

A battle with a Hydra is a battle with the most profound terror of human existence: the ambiguous, complex, uncertain, infinitely variable future.

Before you engage, you won't know the outcome of the struggle. You may win the day easily, with barely a scratch. You may prevail, after much effort and after earning a few battle scars. You may fall, never to rise again.

There may be treasure in the back of the cave, enough to live on in splendor for the rest of your days. There may be nothing.

You may win glory and renown, or be considered a fool, worse off than you were before.

This is the essence of life. The outcome of your actions and decisions is unknown and unknowable.

What separates the adventurer from the bulk of humanity is the willingness to fight in spite of the risks: to meet the enemy on the field of valor, trusting in skill, instinct, and determination to see them through to a good end.

There are no certainties and no guarantees. The hero fights anyway.

So rise, noble adventurer. Take up your sword and torch. Explore the wild, unknown corners of the world. Find hidden treasures and challenge the monstrosities that guard them.

The world needs you.

And as you approach the Hydra, summoning every ounce of your strength, courage, and fortitude, remember one thing.

The moment you lock eyes with the beast, steel your mind, and stand your ground, you earn yourself a place among the heroes of legend, who are honored, first and foremost, for overcoming their own fears.

Fight well, brave soul. I wish you good fortune and every success.

AUTHOR'S COMMENTARY

This book began as a stray thought.

I was elbows-deep in a research-based book on productivity methods. Productivity is a perennial nonfiction topic for a reason: if a few simple recommendations can save hours of wasted effort, banish procrastination, and reduce stress, readers are all ears.

Unfortunately, I couldn't get to the core of the problem. Problems like procrastination and anxiety are universal, but permanent solutions are elusive.

As I toiled over several drafts throughout the course of a year, I came to an unsettling conclusion: it is not possible to solve these problems at the root level. They can't be avoided or made irrelevant by yet another task-tracking method, fancy notebook, software application, habit, or routine. No matter how much we desire certainty, predictability, and guaranteed results, the nature of human existence is fundamentally opposed to any attempt to control what will happen next.

We live in an uncertain, complex, ambiguous, and changing world with shifting demands, unexpected (often unwelcome) developments, and variable rewards. There is no crystal ball to show you the most direct path to victory, and no method of divination to guarantee you'll avoid making costly mistakes.

People strive to make their world comprehensible, predictable, and rewarding, but their locus of control extends only so far. No matter who you are, what you do, or the resources you have at your disposal, you have to learn to live with uncertainty, complexity, ambiguity, and fear of the unknown.

That's the cause of our discontent: we want to be assured of the outcome before we invest. We want to know what's going to happen before it happens, so we can enjoy the good and avoid the bad. We want the maximum rewards for a minimum of effort and cost, and we want the path forward to be clear and unobstructed, free of pitfalls and branching paths. We want the benefits without the risks, without experiencing any form of emotional distress. We want the world to bend to our wishes, but the world is under no obligation to give us what we want.

This is not a comforting line of thought, and insights that make us feel uncomfortable are often difficult to assimilate into our daily lives. We need to consider these factors from a distance, out of the corner of our eye, before we can see how to use them to our benefit.

Fortunately, language gives us a tool custom-built for this purpose: metaphor.

In *Metaphors We Live By*, George Lakoff and Mark Johnson argue that metaphor is at the core of language and perception, both of which profoundly influence our thoughts and actions. The metaphors we use determine how we understand and relate to everything we experience in our daily lives.

Consider Lakoff and Johnson's most vivid example: if "argument is war," that metaphorical framework sets the terms and tone of every step of each subsequent interaction. If "argument is a dance," future conversations will look very different.

There's ample precedent in using metaphor to talk about speculative projects in creative and business endeavors. The best modern example is *The War of Art* by Steven Pressfield.

Pressfield personifies the fear, anxiety, uncertainty, reluctance, and existential dread that accompanies any act of creation as "the Resistance": a malevolent force of nature that has a personal interest in your failure, embarrassment, and permanent disgrace.

Here's how he describes it:

> *Resistance is not a peripheral opponent. Resistance arises from within. It is self-generated and self-perpetuated.* [...]

Resistance is like the Alien or the Terminator or the shark in Jaws. *It cannot be reasoned with. It understands nothing but power. It is an engine of destruction, programmed from the factory with one object only: to prevent us from doing our work.* [...]

Resistance aims to kill. Its target is the epicenter of our being: our genius, our soul, the unique and priceless gift we were put on earth to give and that no one else has but us.

Resistance means business. When we fight it, we are in a war to the death.

This metaphor is useful: it has helped hundreds of thousands of creative people around the world face their fears, summon their courage, and sit down to do their work.

As I sat mulling over my work-in-progress, shortly after rereading *The War of Art*, I had a thought:

What if I start thinking about ambitious, uncertain, speculative projects as some sort of entity, not as an abstract challenge?

What kind of being is frightening, overwhelming, and inherently complex: something that any right-minded person would try to avoid?

I have a deep love of epic fantasy stories, developed over decades of reading sword-and-sorcery novels, exploring virtual catacombs in video games like *Warcraft* and *Diablo*, and playing tabletop roleplaying games like *Dungeons & Dragons* with my family and friends.

The appropriate monster was obvious: the Lernaean Hydra, best known for serving as the second trial of Hercules in Greek mythology.

I began exploring the Hydra as a metaphor for complex projects with unknown and variable outcomes. The thought experiment worked: the metaphor helped me re-examine some of the most difficult challenges involved in acts of creation and investment, and I started taking notes.

The metaphor "projects are Hydras" is a useful way to change the way you think about complex projects and the fundamental nature of every form of creative or speculative work:

- Ambitious projects require that you handle competing demands, which are constantly changing in unpredictable ways.
- Immediate victory is not possible: completing the project requires substantial risk and sustained effort.
- You know it's going to be difficult before you begin, and you prepare accordingly.
- You can't be sure of the outcome until you invest your time and effort, and there is no guaranteed return on your investment.
- The best general strategy is to focus on completing one critical task at a time.

Experienced Hydra-slayers balance the risks against the potential rewards, commit to the challenge even though the outcome is unknown, and focus their attention and effort on what they can control. Courage, valor, fortitude, and persistence are necessary for success.

Instead of being paralyzed by fear and doubt, they develop their skills and abilities, apply them to the task at hand, and commit themselves to the work until it is complete.

That's how professionals in every field of endeavor work: they operate in the same environment of variability, uncertainty, complexity, and ambiguity as seasoned adventurers.

Everything you want to accomplish in life will require you to grapple with the unknown, unsure of the outcome of your actions and decisions. Knowing this in advance makes it easier to keep going when the going gets tough.

In addition, life sometimes forces you to fight battles you didn't ask for: a severe health condition, a natural disaster, the end of a significant relationship, sustained financial hardship, or helping a loved one in crisis. How do you keep fighting when you find yourself trapped in the back of the cave, with a Hydra standing between you and the light beyond?

These matters strike at the core of what it means to be a human being in a complex, ambiguous world: a yearning for growth and progress, but no guarantee you'll be able to attain it.

That's why I decided to explore the topic from the point of view of an experienced adventurer:

- How would they approach such an overwhelming challenge?
- How would they handle the fear and anxiety inherent in the task?
- How would they avoid making preventable mistakes?
- What would they learn to value through hard-won experience?

This book is the result of that exploration.

The Adventurer's advice has roots in a wide variety of fields: behavioral psychology, project management, military doctrine, martial arts, systems theory, and several branches of world philosophy.

How to Fight a Hydra summarizes many of the core ideas from each of these fields. The fictional context allowed me to explore many different applications of these ideas, and use more evocative language and examples. I hope you found the result interesting and useful.

May Fortune smile upon your efforts. Happy adventuring!

PREPARING FOR YOUR ADVENTURE

Keep in mind the following as you prepare to set forth on your own adventures:

1. Uncertainty, complexity, variability, and ambiguity are unavoidable parts of adventuring: you will not be able to guarantee victory in advance. You have to decide on a course of action, prepare as best you can, move forward, and hope for the best.

2. Some people will support your desire to adventure, and others will not. Do not let their doubts and concerns dissuade you if you've decided the experience, benefits, and potential rewards are worth the risks.

3. Every adventurer feels afraid, and has doubts about their ability. That's normal, not a sign of weakness or cowardice.

4. Every adventure requires a certain amount of exploration. You will spend time lost in the wilderness, uncertain about which way to go. You can't eliminate it: exploration is an unavoidable part of adventuring.

5. The struggle will always take longer, and feel more difficult, than you expect. Knowing it's going to be difficult makes it easier to keep going.

6. Stories are embellished to make the telling more interesting: they contain only the highlights, and omit extended periods of trepidation, anxiety, and toil. Take heart: every hero struggles with the same difficulties.

7. The path to victory: keep moving toward your objective, undeterred by hardship.

8. Sharpening your abilities and learning new skills are excellent uses of your time and energy.

9. Take care of your health: perseverance depends on your physical, mental, and emotional fortitude.

10. Experiment with different approaches until you find something that works.

11. Pay attention to your environment, and look for opportunities to put yourself in advantageous circumstances.

12. Confidence is a potent ally: trust your experience, insight, and intuition. Beware the dangers of inattention, impatience, and hubris.

13. Often, the reward at the end of the journey is not what you expect. Be open to the possibility of finding treasure in unexpected places and in uncommon forms.

14. Weigh each new opportunity against your current objective, then decide what to do based on what you value most.

ANNOTATED BIBLIOGRAPHY

If you enjoyed *How to Fight a Hydra* and would like to explore these ideas in more detail, here are a few books you'll find useful:

MEDITATIONS
Marcus Aurelius

Marcus Aurelius was the emperor of Rome from 161 to 180 CE. *Meditations* was not intended for publication: it was a personal journal of his day-to-day observations, thoughts, and difficulties.

Meditations makes it clear that no one is immune to uncertainty, complexity, ambiguity, variability, anxiety, and fear of the unknown: even the most powerful person in the world struggles with these concerns on a daily basis. The best you can do is to act when action is called for, influence what you can, and let go of the things you cannot influence or control.

Aurelius' reminders to himself inspired this book's tone and style. I recommend the Gregory Hays translation, which is clear and easy to read.

THE WAR OF ART
Steven Pressfield

The War of Art is a meditation on the inherent difficulty of creative projects, and "the Resistance" you'll face when you sit down to do your work.

Steven Pressfield, a former soldier, urges you to fight your doubts and inner demons every day.

FEEL THE FEAR… AND DO IT ANYWAY

Dr. Susan Jeffers

In this popular text from the late 1980s, Dr. Susan Jeffers argues that our primary fear is of the unknown and our primary concern is that we won't be able to handle the things that happen to us.

Feel the Fear… And Do It Anyway argues that belief in your ability to handle whatever life throws at you is critical to your well-being and success, and that this belief can be learned and reinforced.

THE BOOK OF FIVE RINGS

Miyamoto Musashi

Miyamoto Musashi was a renowned Japanese swordsman. *The Book of Five Rings*, his treatise on the philosophy and nature of sword fighting, was written sometime around 1645.

Many of the Adventurer's insights on the nature of battle are directly inspired by Musashi:

- Focus all of your attention and effort on cutting the enemy; do not waste time on doubt, anxiety, or unnecessary flourishes.
- Understand the enemy to defeat them.
- Pay attention to the environment, and use it to your advantage.
- Practice and prepare for future challenges with a calm and tranquil focus.

CERTAIN TO WIN
Chet Richards

Certain to Win is a summary of the strategy work of John Boyd, a United States Air Force fighter pilot who was instrumental in establishing the doctrine of "maneuver warfare" currently used by military forces around the world.

Boyd's primary insight relies on the inherent uncertainty, complexity, variability, and ambiguity of combat. If you learn to observe your opponent, environment, and the results of your actions, then re-orient yourself to the present circumstances faster than the enemy, you have a decisive advantage.

This "Observe, Orient, Decide, Act" (OODA) loop is what allows smaller, more agile forces to defeat larger and more formidable adversaries.

Much of the Adventurer's focus on paying attention to the environment, choosing advantageous circumstances to engage the enemy, and experimenting with new approaches to achieve critical objectives is inspired by Boyd.

If you're interested in business or military history, you'll find this book particularly interesting.

THE BHAGAVAD GITA

Translated by Stephen Mitchell

The "Song of the Blessed One" is an ancient epic poem, written in Sanskrit sometime between the fifth and second century BCE in what is now India.

The story takes place on a battlefield. Arjuna, a warrior, is talking with Krishna, his charioteer. Arjuna does not want to fight, even though it is his duty. Krishna reveals himself as a deity and teaches Arjuna about the nature of existence and his place in the cosmos.

Among other things, *The Bhagavad Gita* explores the themes of heroism, duty, and reward:

- Do your duty, even when it is difficult.
- You are entitled to your actions, but not the results of your actions.
- Act, and let go of your concern for the things you cannot control.

Stephen Mitchell's translation is beautiful: less literal than many others, in favor of preserving the verse.

METAPHORS WE LIVE BY

George Lakoff & Mark Johnson

How you think about your situation matters. In *Metaphors We Live By*, George Lakoff and Mark Johnson argue that the implicit and explicit metaphors we use to think about day-to-day situations have an enormous effect on how we approach the world.

Exploring different metaphors can highlight potential errors or biases, and produce useful approaches and insights.

ACKNOWLEDGMENTS

I have had the great fortune of sharing this adventure with a group of renowned heroes, each legendary in generosity and skill:

David Moldawer, gentleman rogue, whose insight and keen perception helped this venture take shape and form.

Lisa DiMona, wise and noble diplomat, whose longstanding counsel and support has made all the difference.

Nora Long, oracle of visions, who saw in early versions of this work the beginnings of a tale beyond my wildest imaginings, then pointed the way.

Carl Rosen, learned sage, whose skill in the arts of bibliomancy brought illumination and clarity to the darkest and most confusing of passages.

Pete Garceau and *Jeff Brown*, master illusionists, who brought spectacular images of the Hydra to life from wisps of pure imagination.

Tim Roven, bard of wonderment, who composed auditory marvels to accompany this work.

Eric Barker, *Tim Grahl*, and *Daniel Rubin*, steadfast rangers who braved early attempts to traverse these unknown wilds, never failing to return with valuable guidance.

James Clear, *Nir Eyal*, *Ryan Holiday*, *Steve Kamb*, *Mark Manson*, and *Shane Parrish*, indomitable warriors whose battle cries inspired courage and fortitude in times of doubt and despair.

Kelsey Kaufman, cleric of the light, whose love and unwavering support makes all things possible.

Lela Kaufman and *Nathan Kaufman*, wild and curious spirits, whose desire for exploration and growth inspires me to adventure.

PRODUCTION NOTES

This book was designed and produced by the author using PrinceXML Book Edition.

princexml.com

The book is typeset in *IM Fell English Pro*, *IM Fell Three Line Pica Pro*, and *IM Fell Flowers*, which were digitally reproduced from the work of Dr. John Fell, a seventeenth century bishop of Oxford, by Igino Marini.

iginomarini.com/fell/

Cover design by Pete Garceau.

petegarceau.com

Audiobook sound design by Tim Roven of Tabletop Audio.

tabletopaudio.com

ABOUT THE AUTHOR

Josh Kaufman is the bestselling author of two previous books: *The Personal MBA: Master the Art of Business* and *The First 20 Hours: How to Learn Anything... Fast!*. His books have sold over half a million copies worldwide, and have been translated into twenty-two languages.

joshkaufman.net
personalmba.com
first20hours.com
howtofightahydra.com

To receive updates and information about Josh Kaufman's latest research and writing, including upcoming books and courses, please visit joshkaufman.net/newsletter

Made in the USA
San Bernardino, CA
31 October 2018